HERCULANEUM

D1415644

Editions KINA ITALIA

© Copyright **KINA ITALIA** / L.E.G.O.
Layout: Renzo Matino - Schio
Printed by: **KINA ITALIA** / L.E.G.O.
Text: Claudia Converso
Translation: A.B.A. - Milan
All right to photographs and text reserved.
Reproduction, including partial reproduction, forbidden

HISTORICAL INTRODUCTION

Just a stone's throw from Naples, on the edge of the town of Resina overlooking the Gulf of Naples, lie the remains of ancient Herculaneum, one of the most important and celebrated archaeological sites in Italy.

According to mythological tradition (reported by Dionigi d'Alicarnasso), the town was founded by none other than Hercules, on his return from Iberia where he performed the tenth of his twelve terrible labours by capturing the flocks of the monster Geryon. The town was thus called Herculaneum by the Romans and Herakleion by the Greeks.

Historically, Herculaneum actually did have Greek origins, of which little trace remains apart from a few metres of the most ancient city walls, and above all the layout of the town; the cardines and decumani (i.e. the main roads running north-south, here parallel to the coastline, and the secondary ones running east-west, here perpendicular to the coast and very steep), built at right angles in a strictly regular pattern, immediately bring to mind the ancient Greek Neapolis.

The Greeks of Neapolis and the other major Greek colony of the area, Cumae (who already controlled nearly all the Campanian coast, from Cumae to the Sorrento peninsula) ruled Herculaneum as from the 6th century B.C.; a century later the Samnites gained control, and the town remained under their domination for centuries. Some interesting inscriptions in the Osco-Samnite language survive from this period.

Between the 2nd and 1st centuries B.C., Herculaneum was one of the Campanian towns which fought against rampant Roman domination in the "Allies' War". This was a hard-fought but vain struggle; in 89 B.C. the town of Hercules, conquered by one of Sulla's legates, was forced to yield to Rome, and subsequently became a Roman municipium, like other defeated towns.

Roman inscriptions relating to this period and mentions by historians suggest that in the century following its conquest, Herculaneum must have undergone a degree of demographic, political and urban development; it also came to the fore in the ambitions of Roman patricians, mainly because of its very mild climate (described admiringly by Strabo) and its enviable geographical position: "oppidum tumulo in excelso loco propter mare, parvis moenibus, inter duos fluvios infra Vesuvium collocatum". According to this ancient description by Sisenna, it was a small town (the urban area must have been equivalent to about a third of the area of Pompeii: around 370 x 320 metres, with a total of 4000-5000 inhabitants) situated on the furthest slopes of Vesuvius on a promontory between two rivers, overlooking the sea to the south (this appearance changed considerably over the centuries, mainly as a result of two events, the eruption of Vesuvius in 79 A.D. and the eruption of 1631, which radically altered the lie of the land, especially by raising it over 20 metres above its ancient level).

Unlike nearby Pompeii, a mainly mercantile town, the economy of Herculaneum was not entirely based on commerce and crafts, although they flourished, as demonstrated by the household articles found. The town was actually a well-known high-class resort which contained many elegant, elaborate patrician residences of numerous types with a wealth of elegant decorations, often situated in panoramic positions on the slopes of the verdant, vineyard-covered hills, which contrasted with the humbler urban dwellings of the plebeians, while there were few buildings destined for business activities.

Pedestrians probably walked quietly along the town's roads, which were not crowded with vehicle traffic used for trade as in Pompeii; life must have jogged on at a fairly gentle, relaxed pace, typical of the towns chosen by the Roman patricians for their leisure time. It was not enlivened by industrial and commercial activities or animated by the socio-political turmoil suggested by the numerous wall inscriptions in Pompeii.

However, in 63 A.D. this development was abruptly interrupted by the disastrous earthquake which devastated not only Herculaneum, but the entire Campania region. The town suffered such serious damage to its public and private buildings that extensive repair work was necessary (as in the case of the Mater Deum temple, the repair of which was ordered by the Emperor Vespasian, as witnessed by an inscription discovered in the town) if not total reconstruction.

However, the earthquake was only the prelude to a far worse catastrophe involving Vesuvius. On 24th August in the year 79 A.D. the town of Herculaneum, some of which was still undergoing work to repair earthquake damage from 16 years earlier, was engulfed by a huge river of mud and debris produced by the terrifying eruption of the volcano, on whose green slopes the town was built. The town was not hit by lava, ash, white-hot rock and lapilli as in the case of Pompeii, but the final effect was not much different; the town was inundated by boiling mud which, as it flowed down the slopes, wiped out much of what lay in its path, penetrating every home, every street, every building, every square.

Another difference from the fate of Pompeii was that the population of Herculaneum probably had time to escape towards the sea; however, for most of the fugitives the attempt to reach safety failed, because a violent tidal wave forced the boats back to the shore, preventing them from gaining the open sea and fleeing the catastrophe. Human remains and the remains of boats have recently been found along the coast, demonstrating the failure of these attempts.

When the eruption ended, Herculaneum was covered with a thick layer of mud (at some points over 10 metres deep) which wiped it out of the history books. Abandoned by all its inhabitants and buried like a precious mummy in an impenetrable sarcophagus, the town was never rebuilt; only later was the more modest town of Resina built at the edges of and partly on the area where Herculaneum once stood.

A BRIEF HISTORY OF THE EXCAVATIONS

Decumanus Maximus: painting of shop

Paradoxically, by one of those inexplicable (and in this case bitter) ironies of fate, it was the very cause of Herculaneum's fate which has preserved the ancient town to the present day. As the mud dried and solidified over the years, it turned into a kind of thick, compact blanket which adhered to every structure and household article (numerous rooms with vaulted ceilings proved to be entirely filled with mud, which poured in through the skylights above like plaster into a cast), thus protecting the relics which escaped the fury of the flood of mud and debris that engulfed the town and preserving (among other things) the upper floors of the buildings, which is unusual in ancient ruins.

Although on the one hand, unlike Pompeii, numerous masonry structures of public and private buildings were seriously damaged by the shock wave (some still showed signs of the damage caused by the previous earthquake, which had evidently not yet been repaired), on the other hand, entire rooms have been brought to light practically intact, not only in terms of masonry, but also of the household furnishings (wall paintings, statues, mosaics, and even furniture).

The fact that the layer of mud has preserved the wood to the present day is particularly important; this material is normally soon destroyed by wear and tear, atmospheric humidity and its own chemico-physical composition unless suitably protected. Thus the visitor can see staircases, partitions and other wooden structures as well as some specimens of furniture.

The entire town was covered by a hard, compact layer whose hardness and strength varied according to the material of which it was composed and its thickness (which ranged between 10 and over 20 metres); this layer also preserved the remains of Herculaneum from the looting suffered by many other abandoned archaeological sites, including Pompeii, over the years.

Excavating under these conditions presents far greater difficulties, which on the one hand discouraged looters and thieves of antiquities, but on the other hand has created many problems for archaeologists who, with an entirely different spirit, have devoted their efforts to rediscovering a town that seemed destined never to see the light of day again.

The existence of Herculaneum was probably not entirely forgotten after the eruption of 79 A.D., at least locally; the inhabitants of Resina may well have accidentally discovered some building or structure of the ancient buried town when digging foundations, canals or wells, but these episodes can hardly be classed as archaeological excavations. The town was mentioned by Sannazzar in his "Arcadia" in 1504. However, it was not until the early 18th century, i.e. after the second devastating eruption of Vesuvius in 1631, that we can strictly speak of a discovery; it was only in 1709 that the Austrian Prince d'Elboeuf discovered the stage wall of Herculaneum's Theatre.

This was also a chance discovery, which took place during the excavation of a well. As often happened during that period, instead of leading to scientific study and research, the dis-

covery gave an aristocratic art lover the opportunity to take what he liked best from the site uncovered, with no concern from the harm that might be caused to the structure. For almost a decade the Theatre was stripped of its marble coverings and numerous statues, later purchased by foreign museums.

Excavations which, while not yet scientific, were at least authorised, were begun on the site in October 1738 by order of King Carlo of Bourbon, who commissioned them from Spanish military engineer Alcubierre. The work, performed by local workmen in accordance with the system of tunnels and shafts, brought to light the entire Theatre and the Basilica, together with the "Villa of Scrolls", with its very important collection of statues and a priceless philosophical library consisting of almost 2000 papyrus scrolls.

With the aid of the Swiss Karl Weber, who among other things drew up a very accurate plan of the Villa of Scrolls, and the Italian Francesco La Vega, who prepared a draft plan of the town, the excavations continued until 1766, when the tunnels were filled in, the shafts used for access to the ruins were closed, and the work was discontinued.

In the meantime, the Royal Herculaneum Academy had been founded in 1755, and produced eight volumes entirely devoted to illustrating the frescoes, bronze statues and scrolls discovered during the early years of the research.

Despite their undeniable importance, the excavations performed by Alcubierre, Weber and La Vega only give a rough idea of what Herculaneum must have been like before the eruption of 79 A.D.

In 1828 the research began again, this time using the more modern method of open-air excavation which had already been tried out and was currently being used in Pompeii. Excavations continued until 1855; during this second excavation period a section of two blocks of dwellings containing a peristyle (a colonnaded inner courtyard) came to light in the Argos House.

Fourteen years later, King Vittorio Emanuele II gave the order that excavation work should recommence. All that was discovered was a portion of two more blocks and the south façade of the Baths, and the digs were interrupted in 1875, partly because of protests from Resina landowners, who had no intention of sacrificing their land to archaeological research.

In view of the difficulties encountered, in 1904 English archaeologist Carl Waldstein suggested setting up an international organisation to direct the excavation work, but his idea came to nothing.

Finally, in 1927, the research recommenced under the direction of the great Italian archaeologist Amedeo Maiuri, who gave it a fully scientific, systematic character, and made discoveries of inestimable value. The work of excavation, restoration, repair and conservation of the material found, which was subsequently carried on by Professor Alfonso De Franciscis, is still continuing today.

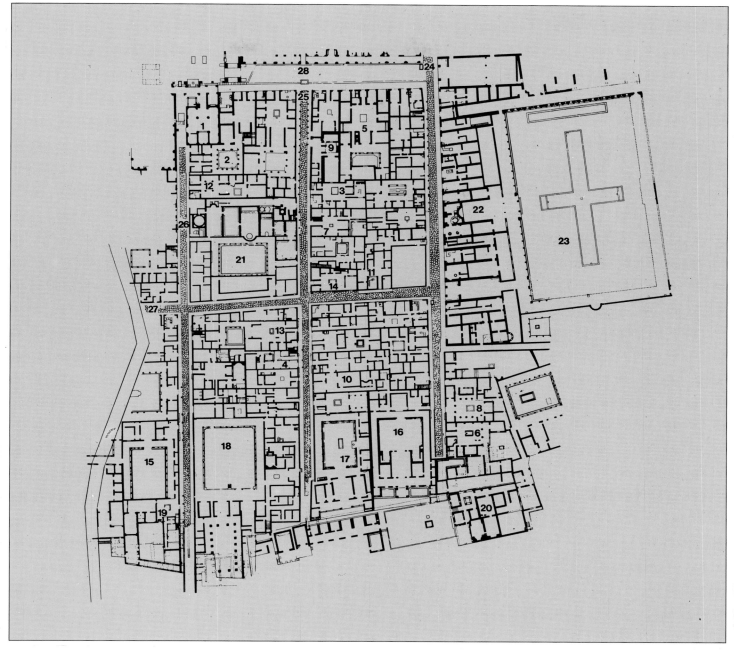

HERCULANEUM
Map of the excavations

1 Aedes Augustalium
2 House of the Tuscan Colonnade
3 House of Neptune and Amphitrite
4 Hurdle-house
5 Bicentenary House
6 Gem House
7 House of the Charred Furniture
8 Telephus Relief House
9 House of the Beautiful Courtyard
10 House of the Alcove
11 House of the Great Portal
12 House of the Double Atrium
13 House of the Wooden Partition
14 Samnite House

15 Argus House
16 Deer House
17 House of the Mosaic Atrium
18 Shelter-house
19 Aristide's House
20 Suburban Baths
21 Central Baths
22 Apsidal Room in the Gymnasium
23 Open Area in the Gymnasium
24 Fifth Cardo
25 Fourth Cardo
26 Third Cardo
27 Lower Decuman Gate
28 Central Decuman Gate and Forum Area

Visitor's itinerary

Access to the excavations is obtained from the entrance on Corso Ercolano, identified by the inscription "Herculaneum". After leaving the ticket office, visitors follow the long viaduct above the archaeological site which gives a splendid view over the Gulf of Naples, and the first overall view of the ancient town and the area in which excavations are still continuing. The strictly perpendicular roads which crossed Herculaneum in accordance with the classical layout of Greek towns (which can be seen in ancient Neapolis, for example) can immediately be identified: the five cardines, running north-south parallel to the coast and the **three decumani** running east-west perpendicular to the coast, with the **decumanus maximus** running north-east parallel to the present Corso Ercolano near the entrance. The cardines and decumani divide the

1) Decumanus Maximus: crossroads with Cardo V
2) View of Decumanus Maximus from above
3) Decumanus Maximus: shops

town into insulae, comparable to city blocks, inside which there might be detached houses or groups of dwellings connected by lanes and small streets.

Continuing along the viaduct, we come to an avenue which curves down to the level of the excavations, passing in front of the seaward façades of the **Deer House** and the **Mosaic Atrium House** (Insula IV). Turn right and continue down to the garden of the **Hotel House** (Insula II), between Cardo III, the closest to the coastline, and Cardo IV, from which the visit begins.

To the left of **Cardo III** is the area of the oldest excavations. This is interesting not so much for the homes and shop buildings found there (mainly damaged both by the excavation of tunnels used in the earliest research and by unfortunate restoration work which has visibly changed their

1) Deer House
2) Cardine III
3) Mosaic Atrium House

1) Argos House
2) Hotel House
3) Hotel House: "balneum"

appearance) as for the presence of the **Argos House** (Insula II, Cardo III, no. 2), a residence which certainly belonged to a wealthy Roman patrician family, whose most interesting aspect is the **portico with columns** and pillars that enclosed the garden on three sides. In addition to this first peristyle, which came to light during the 1828-1855 excavations, there is a second, only partly recovered, running along the garden. The garden leads to a large room (the triclinium) originally decorated by a fresco (now lost) portraying "Io watched by Argos", after which the house is named.

On the opposite side of the road to the Argos House is the **Hotel House** (Insula III: main entrance, **Cardo IV**, no. 19; secondary entrance Cardo III, no. 1); this

dwelling, in a rather poor state of preservation, occupies a large part of the insula it belongs to. As it was the largest house in the southern district and the only one with a private balneum, archae-ologists originally believed that the building was a hotel, hence its name; however, subsequent studies revealed that it was actually a pri-vate house, probably inhabited by patricians.

Continuing along Cardo III we come to the **Skeleton House** (Insula III, Cardo III, no. 3), so called because a human skeleton was found on the top floor in 1831. The building, which consists of three separate constructions, is mainly interesting for the roofed atrium and the two nymphaea, specially built as light shafts to illuminate the various rooms of

the house (which are quite small). Another interesting aspect is the oecus, the typical drawing room of Roman villas, which here has an unusual apsidal ceiling and a beautiful opus sectile floor with multi-coloured inlay decorations. The oecus opens onto a small courtyard decorated with a central basin and embellished by an almost trompe l'oeuil wall decoration portraying a garden.

Turning right at the crossroads of Cardo III and the Decumanus Inferior (where a priceless wooden clothes press was found in a cloth **vendor's shop)** and right again at the crossroads of the latter with **Cardo IV**, we come to the Wooden **Partition House** (Insula III, Cardo III, nos. 11 and 12). The outer façade of this patrician domus, which has a portal and small windows and is fitted with seats, remains intact as far as the second floor. On the right of the atrium, which is very large and has a compluvium roof and marble impluvium to collect rainwater, is a cubiculum (bedroom; there are two

1) Cardo IV
2) Skeleton House: detail
3) Wooden Partition House: garden
4) Skeleton house: sacellum

more, with wooden beds, to the left of the hall) with an elegant mosaic floor and a table supported by a small statue of Attis. The tablinum (the dining room and lounge) leads off the atrium; it was once separated from the hall by the three-leafed folding wooden door after which the house is named. Behind the tablinum is a porticoed garden overlooked by the main room of the house.

Immediately after the Wooden Partition House is the **Grid House** (Insula III, Cardo IV, nos. 13-15), so called after the technique used to build the walls, in which a wooden grid or cane framework was filled with rubble and lime (opus craticium). This is an interesting example of a working-class house consisting of two separate dwellings with independent entrances, which were rented by different families; note the balcony supported by columns which runs along the side overlooking the road.

After passing the **Bronze Hermas House** (Insula III, Cardo IV, no. 16) whose tablinum is decorated by a bronze bust of the owner, we come to the **Mosaic Atrium House** on the opposite side of the street (Insula IV, Cardo IV, nos. 1 and 2). This house, which actually consists of two buildings, is named after the elegant checkerboard patterned mosaic decorating the

1) Wooden Partition House
2) Wooden Partition House: paintings in garden
3) Wooden Partition House: detail
4) Wooden Partition House: atrium
5) Grid House

20

atrium floor. From the hall, through a windowed portico (remnants of whose wooden framework are visible), we reach the garden, overlooked by bedrooms and an exedra embellished with mythological decorations. The other wing of the house is occupied by a series of small rooms with elegant decorations which form a circle around a large triclinium (dining room) with opus sectile floor; the room overlooks a covered loggia which gives onto an open terrace below, overlooking the sea, at each side of which are two more small rooms.

1) Mosaic Atrium House: plan
2) Mosaic Atrium House
3) Mosaic Atrium House: detail
4-5) Mosaic Atrium House: floor
6) Mosaic Atrium House: the punishment of Dirce

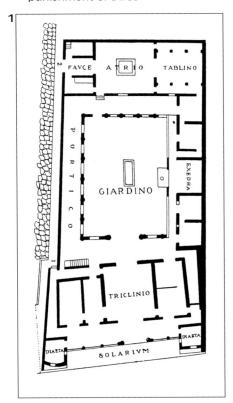

Walking back a little way along Cardo IV, immediately after the crossroads with the Decumanus Inferior, we come to the **Samnite House** (Insula V, Cardo IV, no. 1), so called because it features numerous characteristics typical of the Samnite architecture of the 2nd century B.C., which were maintained by subsequent owners although other elements

1-3) Paintings in Samnite House
2) View of Tuscan-style atrium of Samnite House
4) Large Portal House

Photo on pp. 26-27: Large Portal House - decorations

of the building were partly modified. Entered through a portal decorated with Corinthian capitals, the ground floor of the house consists of a hall decorated with embossed coloured blocks of fake marble in the Samnite style, an atrium with a large marble impluvium to collect rainwater and a gallery with Ionic columns at the upper level, a cubiculum decorated with a fresco portraying "The Rape of Europa", a large drawing room and a tablinum with an elegantly decorated floor.

Next to the Samnite House, on the Decumanus Inferior, is the **Large Portal House** (Insula V, Decumanus Inferior, no. 35), named after the elegant entrance portal surrounded by brick half-columns with Corinthian capitals decorated by "Victories". The

arrangement of the inner rooms, which give onto a roofed vestibules, suggests to experts that the house actually represents a reconstruction of part of the nearby Samnite House carried out during the Imperial age.

After passing the **Fountain of Neptune** at the corner of the Decumanus Inferior and Cardo V, decorated with a gargoyle portraying the Sea God, and, further along on the left, the largest shop found in Herculaneum and the **Fabric House** (so called because pieces of fabric were found in one of its rooms), we come to the **Deer House** (Insula IV, Cardo V, no. 21). Probably built between 41 and 68 A.D., this is one of the most elegant homes found in Herculaneum. The extensive building consists of a large rectangle, the longer side of

1) Deer House: plan
2-3) Views of inner garden of Deer House

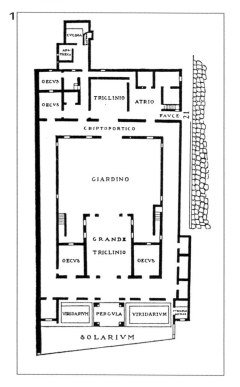

1

2

3

4

5

which measures 43 metres, divided into two areas: a north area comprising the hall and other inhabited rooms, and the south area, consisting of terraces overlooking the sea and connected by a four-sided windowed portico. The roofed atrium, whose walls are decorated by architectural elements against a black background to halfway up and a white background on the other half, leads to the triclinium, outstanding for the elegant marble decoration covering the floor. The sculptured group of "Deer attacked by Dogs" after which the house is named was found in this room. Next, we come to the cubiculum, with its red-painted walls and marble floor, followed by a room with vaulted ceiling decorated in the same way, in which a small statue of a "Satyr with Wineskin" was found. After crossing the large inner garden, around which runs a four-sided windowed portico with mosaic floor and walls decorated with elegant frescoes depicting "Cherubs' Games", we enter the large summer triclinium to the south, at the sides of which there are two small rooms decorated with precious marbles, followed by a loggia with four pillars, also flanked by two rooms, in one of which the statuette of "Hercules Inebriated" was found.

6

1) Deer House: Deer attacked by Dogs
2) Deer House: interior
3) Deer House: detail of mosaics on front of portal
4) Satyr with Wineskin
5) Hercules Inebriated
6) Deer House: painting

After leaving the **Deer House**, walk along the ramp leading to the **Sea Gate**; from here, we enter the southernmost area of Herculaneum, occupied by the maritime district, the remains of which lie near the city walls, between the end of Cardo IV and the end of Cardo V. Some sacelli

Finds of human bones

33

(votive chapels) and a sacred area have been found near Cardo IV; next to it is an open space occupied by the marble base of a statue and a funeral altar bearing an epigraph with an honorary decree. Both were dedicated to the most illustrious citizen of Herculaneum, **Proconsul Marcus Nonius Balbus**, whose statue must have stood on the marble base, now empty (an equestrian statue of the Proconsul is housed in the Naples Archaeological Museum).

1) Swimming pool in "calidarium"
2-3-4-5) Details of baths

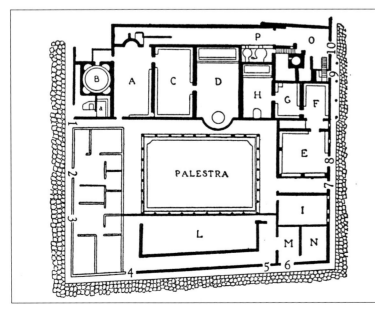

PLAN OF BATHS

1. Entrance to men's baths
2. Latrine
A. Apodyterium of men's baths
B. Frigidarium of men's baths
C. Tepidarium of men's baths
D. Calidarium of men's baths
7. Entrance to palaestra
8. Entrance to women's baths
E. Vestibule of women's baths
F. Apodyterium of women's baths
G. Tepidarium of women's baths
H. Calidarium of women's baths
I. Apodyterium of palaestra
L. Spheristerion
M/N. Rooms associated with spheristerion
9. Ostiary cella
10. Entrance to "praefurnium"
O. Well and water tower
P. "Praefurnium"

Immediately alongside this area are the **Suburban Baths**, probably the best preserved baths of antiquity on the whole (they date from the second half of the 1st century A.D., and are therefore later than the other Baths in Herculaneum; see below). They have a square plan, with an elegant outer portal leading down to a vestibule. The vestibule, illuminated by a light shaft resting on four columns surmounted by twin arches, leads to the various rooms of the Baths, which have marble floors, seats and decorations and even, in some cases, wooden doors and window frames in an excellent state of preservation. The frigidarium, containing the pool used for cold baths, which is still well preserved, like the fistula (water pipe) that supplied it, leads to a room decorated with stucco reliefs portraying warriors. Next, we come to the tepi-

1-2-3) Stucco reliefs of warriors
4) Altar in honour of Marcus Nonius Balbo
5) Gem House

darium, which had a central tank filled with lukewarm water, the laconicum or sudatorium (for steam baths), and finally the calidarium, with its hot-water pool.

On leaving the Suburban Baths, follow **Cardo V** again. We immediately come to the **Gem House** (Insula Orientalis I, Cardo V, no. 1), so called because a gem decorated with the portrait of a women, dating from the age of Claudius, was found in one of its rooms. This is a single house divided into two quite separate areas: the most elegant part, at road level, includes a magnificent atrium decorated with red and black wall paintings, a tablinum, a kitchen, a triclinium with mosaic floor in geometrical patterns, and a terrace overlooking the sea; the part at the lower level, just above the Suburban Baths, is more modest in appearance.

Alongside the Gem House is the **Telephus Relief House** (Insula Orientalis I, Cardo V, nos. 2 and 3), one of the most elegant and spacious in the maritime district. This

1) Sundial
2-4) Telephus Relief House: details
3) Walls and columns of portico of Telephus Relief House, featuring decorations with a red background

two-storey house has a colonnaded atrium with reassembled fragments of two reliefs portraying chariot races; the columns support the rooms on the top floor. From the atrium, a corridor leads to the peristyle, which surrounds a garden embellished by a rectangular basin with blue background situated in the centre. Some rooms which retain part of the original pictorial and mosaic decoration open onto the adjacent open terrace; the most attractive coloured marble house decoration which has survived from ancient times was found in one of them. A smaller room is decorated with a relief portraying the "Myth of Telephus", after which the house is named. At the crossroads between Cardo V and the lane which leads off to the right, we can visit the largest pistrinum (bread-making oven and mill) in the town, which contains two grindstones and various bakery tools (another baker's shop, which belonged to Sextus Patulcus Felix, is situated a few metres further on, between the vestibule and the large apsidal room of the Gymnasium). We next come to the **Gymnasium** (Insula Orientalis II, Cardine V, no. 4), preceded by a large vestibule with two columns. The large unroofed rectangular area, which has not yet been fully excavated, extended for over 80 metres; it was surrounded on three sides by a Corinthian colonnade, and on the fourth side by a cryptoporticus on which the spectators' gallery rested. The colonnaded west wing features a magnificent apsidal room with the grey and white

1-3) Views of the Thermopolium
2) Town bakery
4) Palaestra: detail

4

marble athletes' table in the centre, and two smaller rooms at the sides containing what remains of the original fresco decoration with Egyptian motifs. At the centre is a shallow, cross-shaped swimming pool 35 metres long, which was supplied with water by an elaborate bronze fountain in the middle, portraying a tree trunk around which the Hydra is entwined, with water gushing from its five heads. At the north end of the Gymnasium, near the Decumanus Maximus, is another magnificent vestibule with an opus sectile floor, which almost certainly housed a public gymnasium.**On Cardo V**, opposite the apsidal room of the Gymnasium, stands the **Wooden Sacellus House** (Insula V, Cardo V, no. 31), the most interesting feature of which is the unusual wooden sacellus in the cubiculum which is shaped like a small temple, and was used both as a cupboard and for the worship of the household gods (the Lares).The next house

1-2-3) Details of large palaestra
4) Large palaestra: bronze fountain depicting the five-headed Hydra
5) A statue of the Imperial family standing in the apse

1

2

The **town's Forum** probably stood at the northern end of the Decumanus Maximus, reserved for pedestrian traffic; few traces of it survive, together with a portico which supports two-storey houses. On the left, near the crossroads between the wide street and Cardo III, among various buildings stands the chalcidicum (**portico) of the Basilica,** behind one of the two triumphal arches with four doors and four sides which stood on the Decumanus. To the south, as well as modest homes and shops, there is a square building with pictorial decorations portraying mythological scenes on the walls which must have housed the Curia, or perhaps the ceremonies of public worship of the Lares. The remains discovered on the opposite corner may be the College of Augustals.**Turning into Cardo IV** from the Decumanus Maximus (an **attractive twin-jet fountain with Venus and a head of Medusa** stands on the

1) Black Drawing Room House
2) Decumanus Maximus: fountain of Venus

3-4-5) Black Drawing Room House: details

corner), we can see the Black **Drawing Room House** (Insula V, Cardo IV, no. 11) and, almost

opposite, the Beautiful **Courtyard House** (Insula V, Cardo IV, no. 8). This is a home of modest propor-

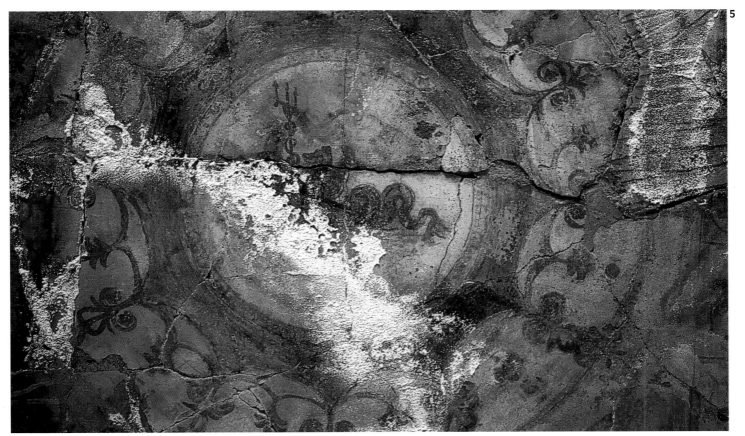

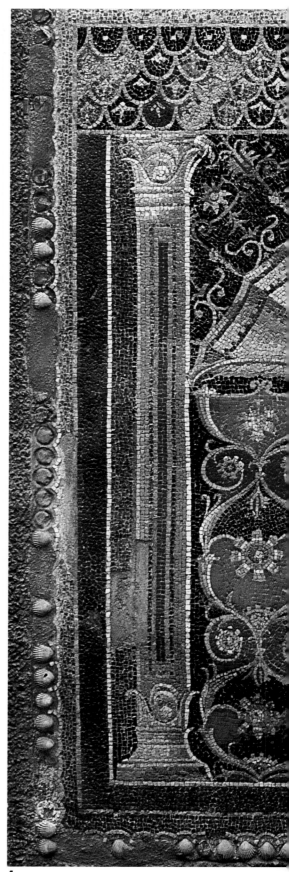

tions with unusually distributed rooms, including a raised courtyard, decorated with an elegant mosaic floor and a staircase leading to the gallery, which features elegant pictorial motifs; numerous remains of furniture and charred wooden sculptures were found in the house.
Walk down the Cardo to the **Neptune and Amphitrite Mosaic House** (Insula V, Cardo IV, no. 7), an elegant two-storey house outstanding for the lovely summer triclinium with a nymphaeum decorated with coloured mosaics portraying, among other things, "Neptune and Amphitrite" and "Hunting Scenes". The shop annexed to the house (entrance at no. 6)

1) Beautiful Courtyard House: detail
2) Beautiful Courtyard House: fresco
3-4) Neptune and Amphitrite House: views of inner courtyard, and mosaic depicting Neptune and Amphitrite

is very interesting; it is one of the best preserved from ancient times, and the wooden structures and many of the furnishings are in perfect condition. Specimens of the goods on sale can be seen on the counter. Next comes the small Charred Furniture House (Insula V, Cardo IV, no. 5), which has a pre-Roman structure dating from the 2nd century B.C. and elegant mosaic and pictorial decorations which are later, probably dating from the age of Claudius. Some wooden furniture (a bed and a table) was found in the house, charred but in an excellent state of preservation, and the beautifully decorated stucco lararium at the end of the inner courtyard is very attractive. On the other side of Cardo IV, opposite the Charred Furniture House and the Loom House (Insula V, Cardo IV, nos. 3 and 4), a **small weaver's shop** where the remains of

wooden material and parts of a loom were discovered, is the entrance to the **Baths**, built around 10 B.C., and redecorated around the mid-1st century A.D. The complex has four entrances: one on Cardo III which gives access to the men's section, and three on Cardo IV. From no. 7, access is obtained to the gymnasium courtyard, from no. 8 to the ladies' section, and from no. 10 to the praefurnium, the room used to heat the water. The ladies' section, which is the smallest and least decorated but has the best preserved structure, opens with a large quadrangular waiting room with a continuous bench running along the walls. This room leads to the a podyterium (changing room), which has a mosaic floor depicting Triton, dolphins and other sea creatures, a stucco-decorated roof, and compartmental shelving where clothes were left. On the left of the changing room is the tepidarium, which also has a mosaic floor with geometrical patterns and

1-2) Charred Furniture House: details
3) Women's apodyterium: mosaic floor depicting Triton
4-5) Women's apodyterium: details

cupboards for clothes. The next room is the calidarium, mainly interesting for the hanging floor which allowed warm air to circulate. The men's section has the gymnasium area in the middle and a peristyle on three sides with a narrow corridor leading off it. The gymnasium led directly to the large apodyterium, with stucco-decorated barrel vaults and a **black-and-white patterned floor, seats installed on three sides,** shelves for leaving clothes on the two longer sides, and a marble tank for ablutions on the end wall in an apse. A passage on the left leads to the frigidarium, where the figures of fish decorating the vault of the dome must have been reflected in the water of the circular pool, with its blue-painted walls, producing a very attractive effect. From here we return to the changing room, which leads onto the tepidarium. This room has a hanging floor as in the ladies' section, and the various furnishings are arranged in exactly the same way; the floor

1) Urban Baths: palaestra
2-4) Men's apodyterium
3) Calidarium (men's section): conch

1

2

52

3

4

is decorated with a mosaic portraying a "Galloping Triton". The calidarium, whose vaulted ceiling is damaged, has a pool which was filled with hot water on one side, and the dais of the labrum (tank for ablutions) on the other side, in an apse.

Leave the Baths by the entrance on **Cardo III** and walk towards the **Decumanus Maximus** as far as the **Double Atrium House** (Insula VI, Cardo III), an attractive two-storey residence with opus reticulatum façade and tufo portal and architrave, which has two atria. The first, which is tetrastyle, continues up to the first floor, while the second, further inside the house, is the Tuscan type, and is interesting for the impluvium, enclosed by a parapet. When the visit to the urban area of the excavations is

1) Double Atrium House
2) Double Atrium House: 4th-style painting with still life
3) College of Augustals: the cella

Photo on pp. 56-57: College of Augustals - detail of interior and commemorative inscription

AVGVSTO SACR
A A LVCII A FILII MEN
PROCVLVS ET IVLIANVS
P S
DEDICATIONE DECVRIONIBVS ET
AVGVSTALIBVS CENAM DEDERVNT

1

over, continue for a short stretch along Corso Ercolano to the area of the **Old Theatre** which, according to an inscription, was built by architect Lucius A. Numisius by order of the duumvir Lucius A. Mammianus Rufus in the Augustan and post-Augustan period. It seated 2000-2500 spectators, and was largely plundered by the Austrian Prince d'Elboeuf, who discovered the stage wall by chance in 1709. Later, starting in 1738, more systematic excavations were conducted by the old tunnel and shaft system under the direction of Marcello De Venuti, but only parts of the complex were uncovered.

2

1-2) College of Augustals: frescoes
3) College of Augustals: painting of
Hercules in the cella

magnificent entrance with colonnaded portico overlooking the sea, which led to the atrium, decorated with an impluvium ornamented with 11 statuettes, and then to the lounge and other rooms that gave on to a first peristyle, including the room destined to hold the library. A second large peristyle (100 x 376 metres) with a large basin in the middle was built around the garden. Priceless marble and bronze sculptures, some of which are now on display at the Naples Archaeological Museum, were found in the gallery and the garden area. From the garden, an avenue leads to a panoramic terrace decorated with an elegant inlaid marble floor.

Frescoes in cella of College of Augustals

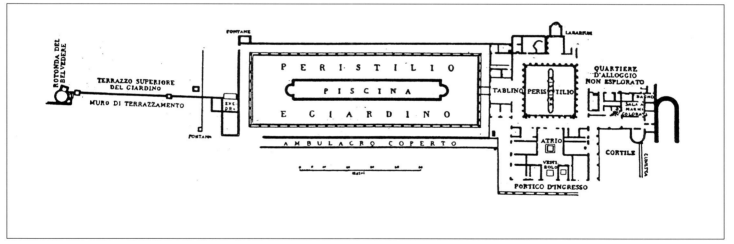

An equally interesting building in the neighbourhood of Herculaneum is the Villa of Scrolls. Found during the 1738-1766 excavations, it contained priceless ancient material consisting of exquisite works of art and a huge library of papyrus scrolls, mainly dealing with philosophical subjects, discovered between 1762 and 1764. The almost 2000 scrolls, found in a charred state caused by a natural chemico-physical process, are now in the Naples National Library. Access to the villa was gained through a

3

CONTENTS